INGLIS ALLEN

OFFICIAL RANGERS ANNUAL 1999

Written by
Douglas G. Russell

Edited by John C. Traynor

Printed and Published by Inglis Allen Ltd.
© 1998 Inglis Allen Ltd. All Rights Reserved.

ISBN 1-89959-904-5

£5.99

CONTENTS

THE BEST OF TIMES

Premier League, 12th April 1998

RANGERS 2   **CELTIC 0**

Thern (25 mins)
Albertz (66 mins)

This was special. Any Rangers victory over their greatest rivals is naturally cause for celebration but, considering the league circumstances prior to this late-season encounter, the end result was quite remarkable.

Consider this. Following drawn games away to Kilmarnock (1-1) and at home to Hearts (2-2), the 'Light Blues' lost 2-1 to Motherwell in

Jorg Albertz scores goal No. 2

mid-March. Obviously, Rangers were not playing well and their Championship dreams, at that stage, seemed dead and buried. However, in a rollercoaster year when almost anything seemed possible in the title race, Celtic arrived at Ibrox in April, surprisingly, still within striking distance, only three points clear at the top. Rangers had to win to draw level but, it should be noted, their opponents were unbeaten in the league in 1998. Victory would require a supreme team effort.

In twenty-five minutes Jonas Thern hit one of the goals of the season. Celtic defender, Rieper, probably believed that his clearing header out of the crowded penalty area was enough to quench any potential danger. On most days, it would have been the correct assumption. However, Jonas had second thoughts and, from all of twenty-five yards, struck a right-foot volley with such precision and power that its ultimate destination was never in doubt.

The unassuming Swede had been criticised from many quarters previously but this day he covered himself in glory. Rangers were now in control but it would be midway through the second period before Ibrox 'Blue-Up' again, following a second goal of real quality that was on a par with its illustrious predecessor.

There seemed to be no imminent danger when Jorg Albertz gathered the ball just inside the Rangers half and moved positively forward. His confidence seemed to grow with every stride and a little burst of pace saw his marker, Burley, fall by the wayside. 'German Jorg' veered left and struck a low shot home from the edge of the box. Once again, the 'Hammer' was responsible for the killer blow.

In truth, Rangers should have increased their tally by two or three more, as further chances were scorned later in the game. Celtic were well and truly beaten.

Players such as Andy Goram, Richard Gough and Brian Laudrup seemed reluctant to leave the field at the end. They knew this had been their last 'Old Firm' encounter and, understandably, wanted to relish the moment a little longer.

Rangers had risen like a phoenix from the ashes of February and March. That was reason enough for celebrations long into the night.

THE BEST OF TIMES

Jorg Albertz ignores the attention of Craig Burley on his way to scoring and celebrates (left).

Jonas Thern hits his 'wonder' strike amd Jonathan Gould is well beaten.

NUMAN AND THE NEW ERA

ARTHUR NUMAN

Just like nearly every other Scot throughout the world with access to a television screen, Rangers fans tuned into the 'Coupe du Monde' in France last summer with eager anticipation.

Naturally of prime concern – well, prior to the Morocco game! – was the performance and possible progress of the National Team but the 'Follow-Followers' were also more than interested in the section involving Holland and the chance to observe Dick Advocaat's first signing for the club.

Twenty-nine-year-old Arthur Numan, Advocaat's captain at PSV Eindhoven for the previous four years, was the established left-back in the Netherlands side and the World Cup competition enabled Rangers fans to see him in action for the first time.

First impressions only reinforced the already confirmed European press opinion that the player was, indeed, one of the finest attacking left-backs around and it would be a privilege to have such an accomplished player at Ibrox. Watching him in the orange (or blue!) of Holland, one particular word came constantly to mind – class. That is, class with a capital 'C'.

Arthur actually began his career as a midfielder but, on the advice of Mr Advocaat, took a step back – obviously in direction only, as the player hasn't looked back ever since! He's come a long way, in footballing terms, since those early days with the Haarlem club in Holland. Naturally, in both the short and long term, Rangers can only benefit from a sportsman who has played regularly and successfully at the very highest level.

By signing the defender, the 'Light Blues' had, at the very least, succeeded in filling a defensive position that caused them innumerable problems the previous year. The fans were sure of that.

A new era had arrived at Ibrox with many changes on the way. Arthur Numan, in a sense, was just the beginning. But what a beginning!

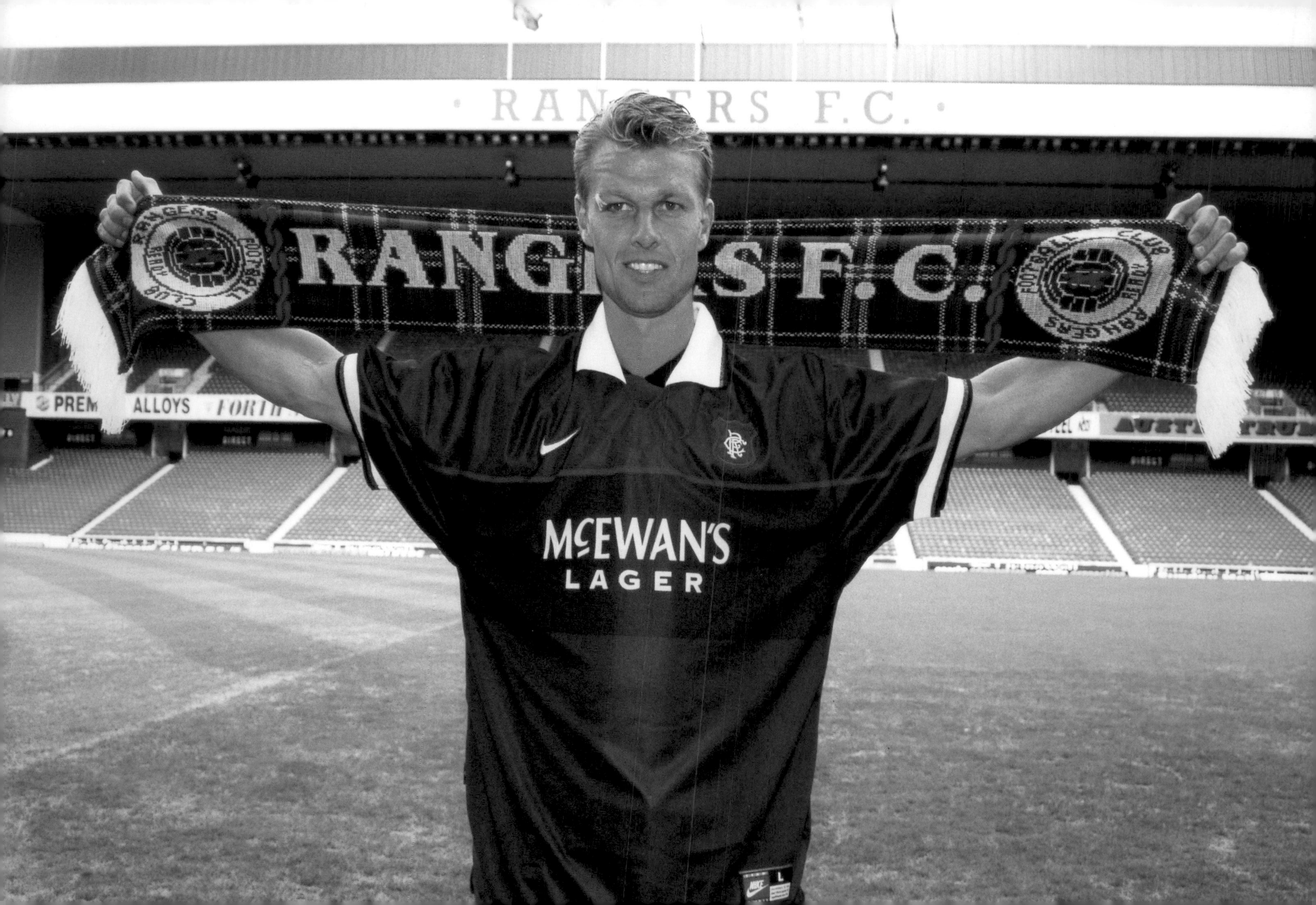
McEWAN'S
LAGER
ALLOYS

GREAT GAMES

AUGUST 1988

RANGERS 5 CELTIC 1

Sometimes we fail to recognise the most significant moments of our lives as they are happening.

  The Rangers fans who had been present at Ibrox on the afternoon of 27th August, 1988 harboured no such thoughts as they celebrated that Saturday evening. This had, indeed, been one of their most memorable days – and they knew it! What they couldn't know, however, was that this highly significant victory over their greatest rivals would not only set them on the road to the Championship but

The 'penalty' that never was at Celtic Park in January, 1998.

also lay the foundations for a glorious nine-year chapter in the club's history.

Yet it all started badly as Celtic, the current champions, went one up within only five minutes of play following a McAvennie goal. Rangers hit back quickly when 'goal king' Ally McCoist fired a superb left-foot strike through a crowded penalty area to equalise. Only ten minutes had been played.

Rangers' second goal of the day is the stuff of legend. A typical long Gary Stevens throw-in from close to the corner flag reached captain Terry Butcher, whose back-header was in turn headed clear of the area by Paul McStay. Ray Wilkins was lurking like a predator just outside the penalty box. To say that his perfectly judged and flighted right-foot volley was exquisite, is an understatement. Certainly, the Celtic 'keeper hardly moved as the ball flew past – an exocet missile heading for its target. He could do nothing but spectate . . . . . . and view with grudging admiration! Rangers were ahead and would not be caught.

Celtic substitute, Derek Whyte, appeared at the start of the second half in place of Tommy Burns in an effort to stem the tide. But this was a flood tide. Soon it was three when, following a McCoist header across goal, the Celtic 'keeper misjudged and allowed the ball to dip under the crossbar. The fourth was a gem – a superb Mark Walters cross being met powerfully by the head of Kevin Drinkell. His first 'Old Firm' game, his first 'Old Firm' goal.

The 'Light Blues' were 4-1 ahead and the question now was: "How many?" An answer was not long in coming. Catching Roy Aitken off balance, Ally pounced and headed for goal before being illegally brought down in the area by the Celtic captain. Before a penalty award could be given, Mark Walters, following up, slotted home the loose ball to take Rangers to five. Although the men in blue eased off after this and could possibly have scored again, the rout was complete and a glorious victory was theirs.

Supporters lingered outside Ibrox long after the sound of the final whistle that Saturday. It had been a magical day and many, many more would follow. As the score spread like wildfire throughout the city, many reactions were the same: "Unbelievable," they said.

But it was more than that. It was perfect.

DOUBLE A

AMORUSO

AMATO

YOUNG BLADE

RINO GATTUSO

Rangers lifted the League Cup in 1975 after beating Celtic 1-0 at Hampden Park. The game's solitary goal – a famous diving header – was scored by a combative, fiery midfielder who was a great favourite with the 'Follow – Follow' Boys. Alex MacDonald was his name.

Some twenty-one years later, young Italian Rino Gattuso arrived at Ibrox fresh from 'Serie B' side, Perugia and with a glowing reputation. By the end of Season 1997/98, the youthful player was already established as a firm favourite with the Ibrox legions, one reason being that, despite his obvious 'non-Govan' background, Rino played for the jersey as if to the manor born. Alex MacDonald with attitude, indeed!

The Italian's uncompromising style of play will not win him many friends in opposition camps but, then again, back in the Souness era, Graham Roberts was never that popular away from Ibrox in his day!

Rino's all-important first league goal in the blue was greeted with an outstanding ovation by the majority of a 49,000 crowd. It came in the 3-2 November home victory over St. Johnstone last season, when a certain Marco Negri scored the other two. Showing a commitment second-to-none that day, the Ibrox masses had been willing the 'Wee Man' to score and he duly obliged.

Months later, in late April 1998, Rangers played a vital league encounter against Hearts at Tynecastle, with so much still at stake. The 'Light Blues' were quite superb that day, notching a comprehensive 3-0 victory over their Scottish Cup Final opponents. Rino Gattuso scored twice and was, in fact, somewhat unlucky not to make it a 'hat-trick'.

Away from Scotland, the youngster is fast becoming a regular in the Italian 'Under 21' squad. Towards the end of last season, he was on the scoresheet when Scotland's 'Under 21' team were beaten 4-0.

Cast your mind back to April 1998. Following two superb victories over Celtic, Rangers suffered a disastrous 1-0 reversal at Pittodrie in the Championship race. As the players left the field, Rino's distress was plain for all to see.

The youngster may well wear his heart on his sleeve but, as the Ibrox fans have often said – "He's one of us".

RINO GATTUSO

FEEL THE FORCE

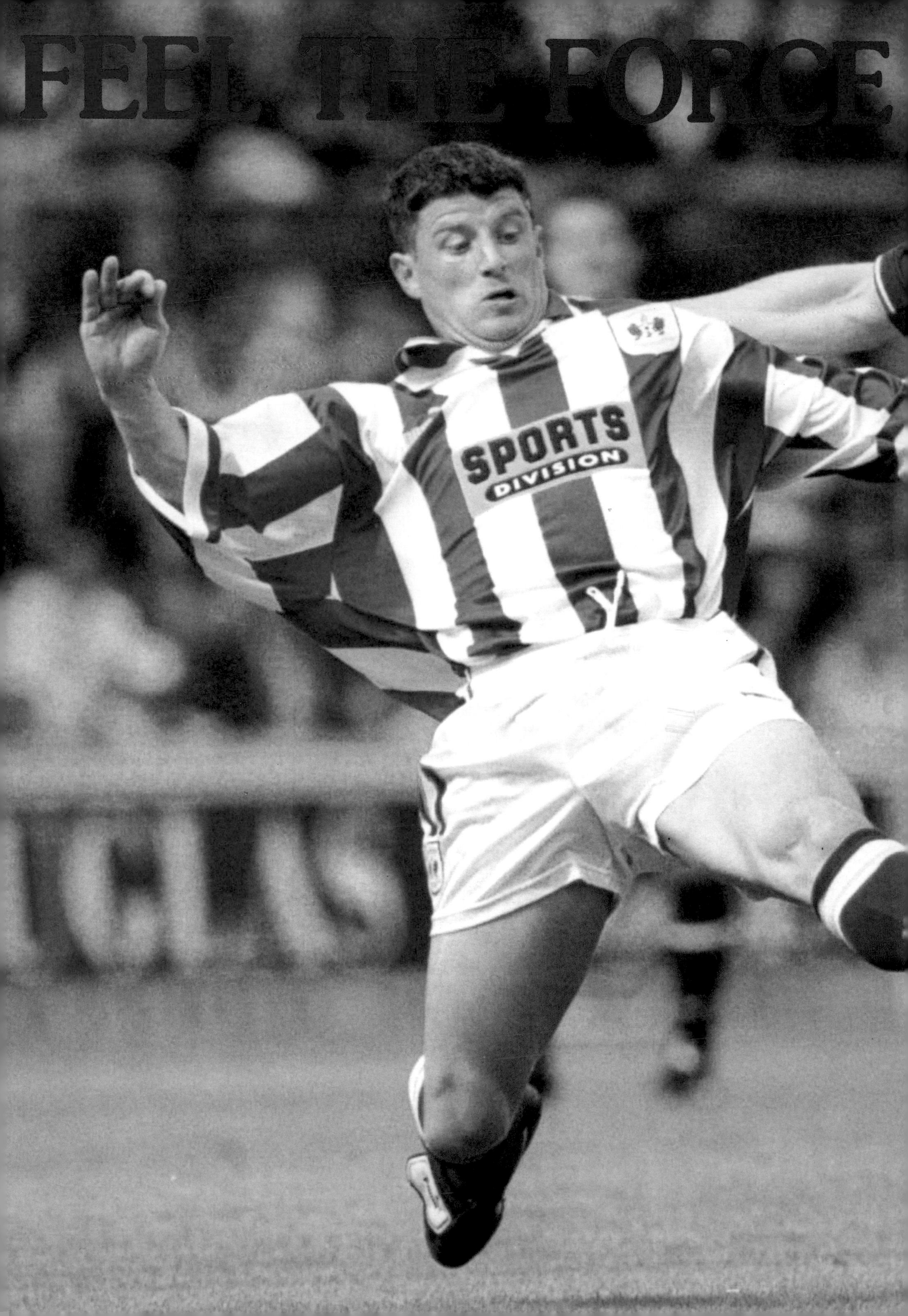

THANKS FOR THE MEMORIES

BRIAN LAUDRUP

It is often said that all good things come to an end. Rangers' 'Great Dane', Brian Laudrup, left the club at the end of Season 1997/98 after four years in Scotland, having signed from Fiorentina in 1994.

Few would dispute that he was not only the most talented footballer to pull on the blue of Rangers in modern times but also a marvellous ambassador for the club. Surely Walter Smith's finest-ever signing.

'Godrup' set the standard way back in August 1994 in his league debut for Rangers, against Motherwell at Ibrox on the season's opening day. With the score 1-1 and the second half slipping away, Brian Laudrup exploded onto the Scottish football scene. A magnificent mazy run from just outside the Rangers penalty area left defenders trailing in his wake as the Dane set up Duncan Ferguson's winner. From then on it just got better and better, with Brian's strike in the 3-1 Hampden victory over Celtic that October, the goal of the campaign for many.

The following season, Laudrup's wonderful Scottish Cup 'semi' goal was only the prelude to a masterly display in the 5-1 demolition of Hearts in the final, when he scored twice and created all three others. That 1996 Cup Final will always be remembered as 'the day of Brian Laudrup'.

Fast forward to November 1996, when he was deployed at Parkhead as a solitary striker ('The Lone Ranger', indeed!) for most of the game. His early goal still separated the teams at the sound of the final whistle. Celtic would have one last chance of stopping their rivals' quest for 'Nine-In-A-Row' when the teams met again the following March for the biggest game in Rangers' recent history. Once again, Laudrup scored the only goal of the game.

In May 1997, the 'Great Dane' was once again honoured by the Scottish Football Writers' Association – the second time in three

seasons. The accolade of 'Player Of The Year' was rightly his. Although his contribution diminished somewhat last year, the memories of those first three seasons will live forever.

In years to come, when today's crop of teenage supporters are older with families of their own, no doubt they will regale their children with stories of the legendary Brian Laudrup.

A player touched by genius.

21

BLUES

ANTTI NIEMI

BROTHERS

ANDREI KANCHELSKIS

Rangers in Europe

1. Rangers were the first British club to reach the final of a European tournament. True or False?

2. Rangers won the European Cup Winners' Cup in 1972. Who did they beat in the semi-final of the competition?

3. Name the scorers when Rangers famously won away to Leeds United at Elland Road in the 1992/93 European Cup.

4. What was so unusual about Rangers' 'home' tie against Vorwarts of Berlin in the European Cup of 1961/62?

5. Rangers played Eintracht Frankfurt in the 1959/60 European Cup and suffered! Can you remember the scores?

6. In a famous victory, Rangers defeated Rapid Vienna 2-0 in Austria in the 1964/65 European Cup. Name the Ibrox legend who broke his leg in the closing minutes.

7. Rangers were unbeaten in the Champions' League, season 1992/93. Can you name the other three top European clubs in their section?

8. Who were Rangers' opponents in the final of the Cup Winners' Cup in 1967 and what was the score?

9. Rangers reached the last eight in the European Cup during the Souness era. True or False?

10. Borussia Moenchengladbach of Germany were opponents at the quarter-final stage of the Cup Winners' Cup in season 1960/61. What was the amazing overall score?

Answers on Page 62

24

THE FUTURE IS HERE

BARRY FERGUSON

Many Rangers fans breathed a sigh of relief when it was confirmed that twenty-year-old Barry Ferguson had finally put pen to paper and signed a new contract which would keep him at the club until the year 2003. It was common knowledge that several top English outfits were waiting in the wings to snap up one of the most naturally gifted Scottish youngsters.

Although only making nine appearances in the Rangers starting line-up last year, the talented midfielder has been more than prominent with the Scotland 'Under 21' squad for some time. Few doubt that, in the very near future, Barry will not only be a lynchpin for the 'Light Blues' but also a <u>full</u> Internationalist.

Of course, at present, the player is still on a learning curve and, as such, will surely benefit greatly under the 'Advocaat' regime at Ibrox. After all, Dutch coaches are renowned for developing young talent on the football field.

Barry's heart is with the club, of that there is no doubt. Thankfully, so now is his future.

25

CELEBRATIONS IN BLUE

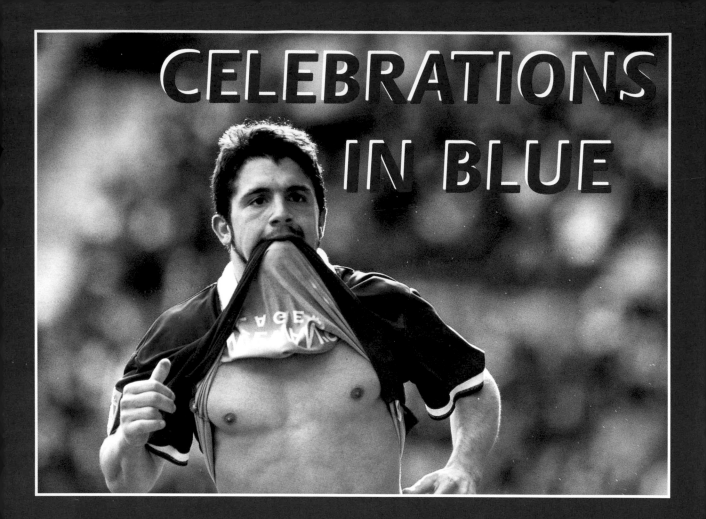

Above left: Rino Gattuso after his second goal against Hearts, 25.4.98.
Above: Jorg and Ally embrace at Parkhead after the strikers' goal, 5.4.98.
Left: Rod Wallace is congratulated after scoring against Motherwell, 15.8.98.
Here: Albertz, Thern and Amoruso after Rangers 2-0 victory over Celtic, 12.4.98.

THE NATURAL

LORENZO AMORUSO

At last it seemed that a natural successor to departing club captain, Richard Gough, had been found.

Following his £4.5 million transfer from Fiorentina, Italian Lorenzo Amoruso arrived at the club last June. That sunny Glasgow day, surely nobody realised it would be all of ten long months before the Rangers fans greeted his competitive debut.

As if major 'achilles' problems were not enough, the player suffered further injury in February, whilst training with the squad. It was felt by many that this was the end of his season.

Eventually, however, though not fully fit, Lorenzo was listed as substitute for the all-important Scottish Cup semi-final against Celtic at Parkhead. After only nineteen minutes, he was called into the fray as Gordan Petric left the field. The 'Blues Brothers' greeted his arrival with acclaim – they had, indeed, waited a long time.

The 'Big Man' played his part in a famous victory, seeming to grow in stature as the game progressed. He even tested 'keeper Gould with a thunderous forty-yard strike for good measure!

The following week, Amoruso played from the start at the heart of the Rangers defence, again versus Celtic, but this time at Ibrox. The home side's first goal, courtesy of Jonas Thern, followed a hoisted free kick from the Italian. Nobody celebrated more at the end of the ninety minutes.

Perhaps more than anyone, Lorenzo Amoruso deserved some joy at the end of his frustrating first year in Glasgow – but it was not to be. There would be no League or Scottish Cup triumph for him this time.

One thing was certain, however – the possibility existed of building a new 'Iron Curtain' defence, with Amoruso at its heart.

Now, there's a thought.

LORENZO AMORUSO

THE TRUE THERN

JONAS THERN

Much was expected of Jonas Thern when he arrived at Ibrox at the beginning of last season from 'Serie A' club, Roma. Understandably, because, in addition to his years playing at the top in Italy, the Swede had also been captain of his country. Not a bad pedigree!

Early on, however, little seemed to go according to plan, as a series of niggling injuries plagued his first few months at the club. Even when playing, Jonas never seemed to be 100% match fit.

By the player's own admission, it was really only after January 1998 that he felt truly fit enough to fill the demanding midfield role, as required. Since that time, the 'Follow-Followers' have seen the emergence of a totally different player – the 'True Thern'.

His first goal for Rangers was the crucial equaliser away to Kilmarnock in February. Then he scored three times in three consecutive

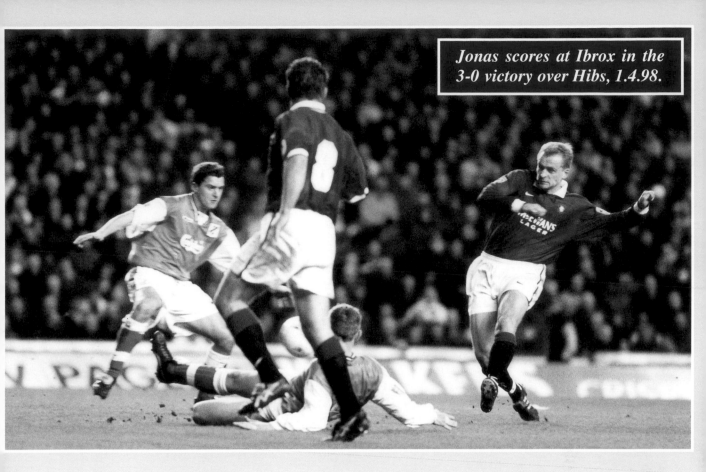

matches against St. Johnstone (home), Dunfermline (away) and Hibernian (home), with the superb strike in Fife being particularly impressive. But the best was yet to come . . . .

Celtic arrived at Ibrox in April three points ahead of their greatest rivals in the Championship saga, knowing that a draw at this late stage of the season would be no great tragedy. Rangers, however, had to win, of that there was no doubt. Step forward, Jonas Thern.

Lorenzo Amoruso's free kick deep into the Celtic box was headed cleanly away by Marc Rieper and bounced just in front of the Swede some twenty or so yards out. In the blink of an eye, his thunderous right-foot volley was buried beyond Gould in the Celtic goal. Reminiscent of that famous Ray Wilkins strike in the 5-1 victory of August '88, this was indeed something to savour! Rangers were now in full flight and victory would be theirs.

Sadly, injury again was to play a part and Jonas would miss those two final, crucial league games of the season and the Scottish Cup Final as well.

The latter part of the campaign confirmed, at least, the importance to Rangers of a fully-fit Jonas Thern – the 'True Thern' in every sense.

COLIN HENDRY
RANGERS

AND

SCOTLAND

TRIUMPH IN EUROPE

THE 1972 CUP WINNERS' CUP

Season 1972/73 could hardly have started so badly for Rangers – they lost three times to Celtic in the space of one month in August/September. Several months later, however, after a quite magnificent European run, the 'Light Blues' would be only one game away from their greatest triumph.

This was not the first time that Rangers had been on the verge of European glory as, in both 1961 and 1967, the Ibrox club lost in the final of the Cup Winners' Cup to Fiorentina and Bayern Munich respectively. So tantalisingly near, yet so frustratingly far from the ultimate victory.

The path to the final that year was certainly no easy passage, with top-class opposition from France, Portugal, Italy and Germany waiting in the wings. French outfit, Rennes, were beaten 2-1 in the first round before the draw paired Rangers with the might of Sporting Lisbon.

A slender 3-2 lead was taken to Portugal, where the home side recorded the same scoreline. Both teams then notched another in extra time. It was only after losing the penalty shoot-out that Rangers were awarded the tie – the referee having finally been convinced that the 'away goals' ruling applied.

Following a 2-1 aggregate victory over Torino of Italy in the next round, Rangers then faced the powerful German representatives, Bayern Munich, in the semi-final. The Scots, having drawn 1-1 in the 'Fatherland', overwhelmed their illustrious opponents 2-0 at Ibrox in front of 80,000 delighted fans and Barcelona beckoned. In late May, over twenty thousand men and boys, decked out in blue, headed

The replica of the European Cup Winners' Cup which is on permanent display in the Ibrox Trophy Room.

for Spain and a date with destiny.

Moscow Dynamo were the first Soviet team to reach the final of any European competition and were worthy opponents. The 'Light Blues' led 2-0 at the interval and, when a third followed early in the second half, it seemed to be all over as celebrations began. To their credit, the Russians fought back to score twice and thus ensure a nervous final few minutes.

As history records, Rangers held out for the most famous of victories and European silverware would soon grace the Ibrox Trophy Room.

The Campaign Pennants

THE EUROPEAN CUP WINNERS' CUP

FIRST ROUND:

1st Leg	Rennes 1	Rangers 1
		Johnston (68)
2nd Leg	Rangers 1	Rennes 0
	MacDonald (38)	

SECOND ROUND:

1st Leg	Rangers 3	Sporting Lisbon 2
	Stein (9 & 19),	
	Henderson 28	
*2nd Leg	Sporting Lisbon 4	Rangers 3
		Stein (27 & 46),
		Henderson (100)

*After Extra Time (Rangers won on "away goals" rule)

QUARTER FINAL:

1st Leg	Torino 1	Rangers 1
		Johnston (12)
2nd Leg	Rangers 1	Torino 0
	MacDonald (46)	

SEMI-FINAL:

1st Leg	Bayern Munich 1	Rangers 1
		Zobel, o.g. (49)
2nd Leg	Rangers 2	Bayern Munich 0
	Jardine (1),	
	Parlane (23)	

The Bayern team included Beckenbauer, Müller, Maier, Roth, Breitner and Höeness, all six of whom would some weeks later be in the West German team which won the European Championship in Brussels, defeating the U.S.S.R. 3-0.

FINAL:

Rangers 3   Moscow Dynamo 2
Stein (24),
Johnston (40 & 49)

Nou Camp Stadium, Barcelona
May 24th 1972. Attendance 35,000

Rangers: McCloy; Jardine, Mathieson; Greig, Johnstone, Smith; McLean, Conn, Stein, MacDonald, Johnston.

RANGERS v. SHELBOURNE
UEFA Cup,
July 1998.

SEASON 1988-89

	P	W	D	L	F	A	Pts
Rangers	36	26	4	6	62	26	56
Aberdeen	36	18	14	4	51	25	50
Celtic	36	2	14	11	66	44	46

Championship secured at Ibrox on April 29th with 4-0 victory over Hearts. Kevin Drinkell and Mel Sterland (remember him?) both scored 'doubles' that day. Season also included 5-1 and 4-1 thrashings of Celtic.

SEASON 1989-90

	P	W	D	L	F	A	Pts
Rangers	36	20	11	5	48	19	51
Aberdeen	36	17	10	9	56	33	44
Hearts	36	16	12	8	54	35	44

The year of Maurice Johnston. Although Trevor Steven scored the title-winning goal at Tannadice in April, 'Mo' was the club's top scorer with 15 goals.

SEASON 1990-91

	P	W	D	L	F	A	Pts
Rangers	36	24	7	5	62	23	55
Aberdeen	36	22	9	5	62	27	53
Celtic	36	17	7	12	52	38	41

Walter Smith became manager after Graeme Souness left to join Liverpool. Mark Hateley joined from Monaco and earned his place in Ibrox legend on the last day of the season when his two goals snatched the title from Aberdeen.

SEASO

	P	W
Rangers	44	33
Hearts	44	27
Celtic	44	26

Rangers secured thei Cup 'double' since 1 became the first Sco Boot'. Understandab with 34 goals.

SEASO

	P	W
Rangers	44	33
Aberdeen	44	27
Celtic	44	24

One of the great sea close to European glo in the 'Champions L an amazing 34 goals domestic 'treble'.

SEASO

	P	W
Rangers	44	22
Aberdeen	44	17
Motherwell	44	20

Not only was Mark H goals) but he became the Football Writers' January 1st saw Rang after only half an hou

-ROW'

1991-92

		L	F	A	Pts
	5	5	101	31	72
	9	8	60	37	63
	0	8	88	42	62

t league and Scottish
Ally McCoist
win Europe's 'Golden
was top scorer –

1992-93

		L	F	A	Pts
	7	4	97	35	73
	0	7	87	36	64
	2	8	68	41	60

as Rangers came so
with an unbeaten run
e'. Ally again notched
Rangers secured the.

1993-94

		L	F	A	Pts
	4	8	74	41	58
	1	6	58	36	55
	4	10	58	43	54

y top scorer (with 22
first Englishman to win
r of the Year' award.
3-0 ahead at Parkhead

SEASON 1994-95

	P	W	D	L	F	A	Pts
Rangers	36	20	9	7	60	35	69
Motherwell	36	14	12	10	50	50	54
Hibernian	36	12	17	7	49	37	53

The year of 'Player of the Year' Brian
Laudrup, one of the most talented footballers
ever to wear Rangers blue.

SEASON 1995-96

	P	W	D	L	F	A	Pts
Rangers	36	27	6	3	85	25	87
Celtic	36	24	11	1	74	25	83
Aberdeen	36	16	7	13	52	45	55

Although Celtic pushed Rangers hard all
season, another domestic 'double' was
achieved. All year the Gascoigne/Laudrup
combination was quite irresistable.

SEASON 1996-97

	P	W	D	L	F	A	Pts
Rangers	36	25	5	6	85	33	80
Celtic	36	23	6	7	78	32	75
Dundee Utd.	36	17	9	10	46	33	60

It was fitting that Brian Laudrup's goal in the
1-0 Tannadice victory should secure the
championship. Once again, it had been, without
a doubt, his season. 'Nine-In-A-Row' – at last!

NEVER SAY DIE

Scottish Cup Semi-Final, 5th April 1998

CELTIC 1

RANGERS 2
McCoist (75 mins)
Albertz (88 mins)

O f course, it had to be Ally – somehow the script was written that way. It must be said, however, that after the first forty-five minutes, the story unfolding was an entirely different one . . . . . .

Celtic, with most of the play in the first half, were the team creating all the chances. In truth, Rangers were most fortunate still to be level as the teams left the field at the interval.

Whatever was said in the dressing-room, it was certainly a rejuvenated 'Light Blue' side that started the second period and, at last, began to play. Both Brian Laudrup and Jorg Albertz brought out good

GOAL No. 1

GOAL No. 2

saves from 'keeper Gould before that man McCoist chose his moment. The build-up was deceptively simple – Jonas Thern hit a cross-field ball to Jorg wide on the left. The German then delivered a low cross into the box that bounced once before 'Super' headed home. Defender Rieper had been taken by surprise when Ally stole in front of him – after all, the striker appeared 'out of the blue'!

After so many years, Jimmy McGrory's amazing record of twenty-seven 'Old Firm' goals had finally been equalled by Rangers' own legend.

The 'Light Blues' were now in total command, with both the German and the Dane going close – but the score still remained at 1-0. That was enough for the all-singing, all-dancing visitors but Jorg Albertz, the magician, had one final trick to perform. With only two minutes remaining, he surged forward from his own half, deeper and deeper into enemy territory, past Lambert to the edge of the box. Following a delightful feint, Rieper was committed and 'Gorgeous George' was faced with only the Celtic 'keeper to beat. He did not fail.

Although Celtic scored deep into injury time, it made little difference as the damage had been done. The Parkhead side's bid to win their first 'treble' in twenty-nine years was at an end. Earlier that year, many had written off a certain Mr McCoist, saying that his career at the top was also at an end. Not for the first time were the doubters proved wrong.

Ally McCoist and Rangers – never say die.

1. Who scored for Rangers in the opening league game of the season?

2. Dundee United were beaten 5-1 at Ibrox in August. What was so special about this result?

3. Jonas Thern and Lorenzo Amoruso signed from which Italian clubs?

4. What was Rangers' biggest victory of the season?

5. Rangers scored more goals than any other team in the Premier Division. True or False?

6. Apart from Marco Negri, only one other player reached double figures in the league scoring charts. Who was he?

7. Can you name the only visiting team to score three times at Ibrox in the season?

8. In the two games against IFK Gothenburg in the European Cup, Rangers only scored one goal. Name the scorer.

9. Rino Gattuso scored twice in late April against which team?

10. Which of Jorg Albertz' two goals against Celtic in the league and Scottish Cup was most special?

Answers on Page 62

Name the Rangers player seen with Paul Lambert (then with Motherwell). Clue: He patrols the same area of the park as Lambert.

Ian Ferguson tangles with a Hearts player who wore the blue to great effect. Clue: In July 1989, he caused a sensation.

BLUES

ROD WALLACE

BROTHERS

**GIOVANNI
VAN
BRONCKHORST**

FLASH GORDON

GORDON DURIE

Injuries are 'part and parcel' of any professional footballer's career. Although all players grudgingly accept them as an aspect of the job, needless to say, some injuries are more worrying than others. Any clash of heads, for example, is always of major concern, for obvious reasons.

As Gordon Durie lay motionless on the rain-sodden Rugby Park turf last February, everybody was anxious. The player had crumpled into a heap with no-one near him, the 'after effects' of an earlier clash of heads. When Gordon was stretchered off, still not moving, players and fans alike feared the worst.

Thankfully, although unconscious for some time, no permanent damage resulted but, because of the potentially serious nature of the injury, Gordon would not play again until April!

There can be no doubt that Rangers missed his strong running and powerful presence – the Ibrox club did not win any of their next three games.

Probably his finest hour in the blue that season was against Hearts at Tynecastle just prior to Christmas. At that stage of the Championship race, the Edinburgh side sat proudly at the top of the league, one point ahead of Rangers, with Celtic two points adrift. Victory was crucial for the 'Light Blues' to regain pole position.

Gordon scored a 'hat-trick' in Rangers' crushing 5-2 Gorgie Road annihilation. It was probably an early Xmas gift to the always loyal 'Follow-Followers'.

For many, memories of another Durie trio came flooding back – his goals in that wonderful 1996 Scottish Cup Final, when 'Jukebox' (with a little help from his friend, Brian) buried Hearts.

In the summer of 1998, Gordon Durie was the only Rangers player to set off for France with the Scotland World Cup Squad. There was concern during the first game, against reigning champions, Brazil, when the player fell to ground clutching his head. Although thoughts of that Kilmarnock night came to mind, no serious damage was sustained this time round and Gordon soon recovered.

GORDON DURIE

Season 1998/99 presents new challenges both to Rangers and the playing staff. It is reassuring to know that Gordon's back – hopefully back for good.

GREAT GAMES

MAY 1991
RANGERS 2   ABERDEEN 0

The signs looked bad, extremely bad, for Rangers prior to this Championship decider and last game of season 1990/91.

Following a disastrous 3-0 defeat at the hands of Motherwell the previous week, the 'Light Blues' title hopes and 'Three-in-a-Row' dreams were seriously in doubt. Visitors and fellow contenders, Aberdeen, required just a draw to lift the title and, in fact, had dropped only one point since 19th January. Obviously, the form team. Rangers' situation was certainly not helped by a horrendous list of injuries which included key players such as Richard Gough and Trevor Steven.

Ibrox Stadium had not known such tension for a long time as the teams kicked off. Aberdeen missed a good chance minutes before Rangers' full-back, Tom Cowan, was stretchered off with a broken leg. A less than 100% fit Ian Durrant took his place. Then, just before the interval, came the moment when a certain striker would carve his name into the history books.

Following Mark Walters' high cross, 'Hitman' Hateley soared above the red defence to bullet home one of the all-time-great headed goals scored by a Ranger. After a difficult first season at the club, Mark Hateley was now on his way to becoming a legend.

The same player scored again early in the second half when he slotted home from close in after 'keeper Watts had failed to hold a Mo Johnston shot. With twenty minutes remaining, John Brown was carried off to be replaced by another barely fit player, Ally McCoist!

Aberdeen poured forward in an attempt to salvage that crucial point but Rangers' walking wounded miraculously held firm. In fact, they ended the game with a back four of Nisbet, Stevens, Spackman and Hurlock – all playing out of their normal position!

Against all the odds, the 'Light Blues' had triumphed and Championship No. 41 was secure. It is worth remembering the thirteen heroes that day – Woods, Stevens, Cowan (Durrant), Nisbet, Spackman, Brown (McCoist), Hurlock, Ferguson, Hateley, Johnston and Walters.

The glory was all theirs.

A LIGHT SHINING

IAN FERGUSON

Football can be a cruel master. Certain players tend to be criticised regardless of their contribution. Even if they are playing well, inevitably the knockers will find fault and pass vocal judgement.

Ian Ferguson always seems to receive far more criticism than he is due. The powerful midfielder played his 300th game for Rangers against Dundee United on that fateful last game of the season in May 1998. It was not to be 'Ten-In-A-Row' and few felt the bitter disappointment more than him.

It had been a frustrating year for the player, with relatively few appearances in the Rangers starting line-up. However, his commitment to the cause remained as strong as ever. Who can say how long Ian Ferguson will wear the blue of Rangers? That is open to debate, as it is with all players.

One thing is certain, though. His light shines in just one direction . . . . and its beam is solid blue.

YOUNG

BARRY FERGUSON

BLADES

CHARLIE MILLER

FOREVER BLUE

RICHARD GOUGH

Although Season 1997/98 ended without a first-team trophy for Rangers, it was supremely appropriate that Richard Gough should have led the club to that historic "Nine-In-A-Row' Championship the previous year. In that final record-breaking period, the defender had played a true captain's role – always leading by example. Let us not forget him.

Richard had become Rangers' most successful captain since the legendary Davie Meiklejohn, who guided the club to twelve league titles way back in the 1920's and 1930's. His place in Ibrox legend is written in stone. Richard Gough now stands comparison.

The player had, indeed, come a long, long way since his first game

Richard celebrates his goal against Celtic in the 2-0 victory at Ibrox, 8.11.97.

for Rangers (surprisingly, against Celtic) back in October 1987. Graeme Souness paid a then club record of £1.5 million to Tottenham Hotspur for his services. Has it really been eleven years?

Years of more than just a few memories . . . . his first goal (and game) in the light blue, when that dramatic last-minute equaliser against Celtic at Ibrox secured a 2-2 draw . . . . scoring the winner in the 1990 League Cup Final against Celtic after having taken on the club captaincy from the departing Terry Butcher . . . . the memorable Scottish Cup achievement in 1992 which laid to rest an eleven-year hoodoo. The list goes on and on.

Needless to say, however, the hopes and dreams of all fans lay in Season 1996/97. Once again, Richard Gough did not disappoint. His return to the Rangers rearguard before the vital Parkhead league encounter in March was crucial, as, without him, the club had suffered defeat at the hands of Celtic (Scottish Cup) and Dundee United (home league match). History shows that Rangers won the day.

Of course, it was sad to see such an illustrious career come to an end – but end it must, as nothing is forever. For the departing hero, America beckoned once more as Rangers welcomed a new era. Although gone, Richard Gough is not forgotten.

In truth, never forgotten.

THE ITALIAN WAY

SERGIO PORRINI

Some players relish pre-season training whilst others struggle to prepare the body for those arduous months ahead. Be that as it may, Sergio Porrini was enjoying this period in the summer of 1998 before the commencement of a most important campaign for Rangers in the so-called 'New Era'.

Coaching systems naturally vary from country to country (even club to club!), so it was reassuring for Sergio to find that the method now installed at Ibrox by Dick Advocaat had a familiarity about it. This type of disciplined and ordered training was similar to the successful system appreciated by the player at Juventus under coach Marcello Lippi. It was 'Serie A' all over again . . . well, apart from the lack of sun!

Sergio Porrini (and fellow-countryman, Lorenzo Amoruso) joined Rangers prior to Season 1997/98 with high hopes of a successful first year at the club. Alas, it was not to be a League Championship triumph or Scottish Cup victory this time round as the 'Light Blues' failed to win a first-team trophy for the only time since Season 1982/83.

Naturally, it had been a frustrating period for the likeable Italian but, nevertheless, the defender still turned in a series of solid performances throughout the campaign – even though, on several occasions, he was played out of position.

Sergio's first goal for Rangers came in the 2-2 draw with Motherwell at Ibrox in late September, 1997. In that first season, three others followed – against Kilmarnock (4-1, November 1997), Aberdeen

SERGIO PORRINI

(2-0, January 1998) and Dunfermline (1-1, February 1998), the strike against Aberdeen being of particular importance.

In many ways, his career is only just beginning at Ibrox, with all the changes that have occurred both on and off the park. Make no mistake, this defender is more than capable of meeting the new challenges that lie ahead.

It is worth remembering that Sergio was a European success with Juventus prior to signing for Rangers. That is success at the <u>highest</u> level.

Nuff said!

THE HAMMER

JORG ALBERTZ

A simple survey – ask any Rangers fan for a personal list of highlights from Season 1997/98. Topping any chart would surely be the German's stunning goals against Celtic, two weeks in a row in April.

Venue No. 1 was Parkhead and the Scottish Cup semi-final tie. After a goalless first half, 'Super' Ally had put Rangers ahead with fifteen minutes to go, when he sneaked in front of defender Marc Rieper to head home Albertz's bouncing cross from the left. This was the striker's 27th 'Old Firm' goal.

As 'you cannae hear the Celtic sing' reverberated around the ground, the celebrating fans would never have believed that the best was yet to come. It happened with only two minutes remaining. Gathering a loose ball just inside his own half, Jorg Albertz strode purposefully

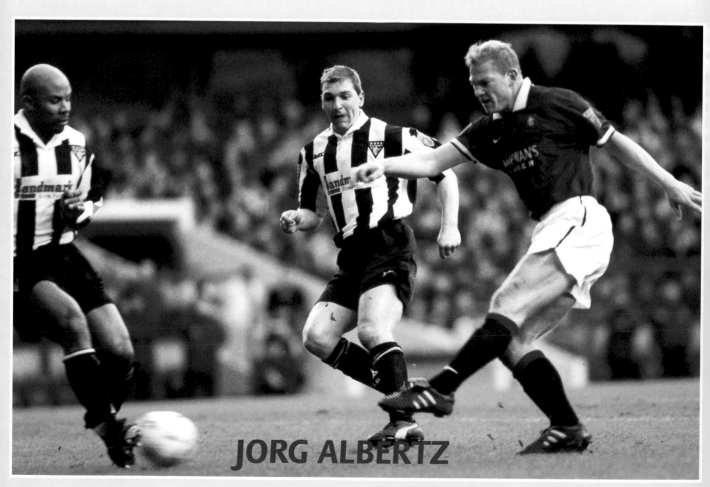

JORG ALBERTZ

forward deep into Celtic territory as the green rearguard retreated. Past the shadowing Lambert and into the penalty area where, despite a lunging effort from Rieper, the German unleashed an unstoppable left-foot drive past the despairing Gould in full view of the travelling Rangers support. How they danced! A goal of real quality had secured a famous victory.

One week later at Ibrox, in the final 'Old Firm' clash of the season, league points were at stake. This time round, the 'Light Blues' had already established a 1-0 half-time lead courtesy of Jonas Thern (more of his thunderous strike elsewhere in the Annual!) before Jorg struck in sixty-six minutes. In many ways, it was a re-run of his goal seven days earlier.

As the snow fell (on a typical Glasgow spring day), the former 'Bundesleague' player won the ball from Lambert and on receiving a short Durie pass, set off for goal, being tracked by Craig Burley. The Celtic midfielder was easily brushed aside before Albertz struck a low left-foot shot from the edge of the box, despite the close attention of Alan Stubbs. The ball nestled comfortably in the bottom corner of the net with Gould beaten for the fourth time in a week. Ibrox erupted as Rangers returned to the top of the league, albeit on goal difference of only one.

Despite the fact that Jorg had his critics during the season, his contribution was vital. The 'Hammer' had notched several important goals that year, with one being remembered as particularly sweet. With only three minutes to go at Easter Road in February and a 1-1 scoreline, he steadied himself some twenty-five yards out and unleashed a terrific shot which arced over Bryan Gunn and dipped into the net. Victory was secured.

However, most 'Blues Brothers' will always remember a certain free-kick on a cold January night at Ibrox in 1997 on the road to 'Nine-In-A-Row'. It is still easy to visualise that five-man Celtic defensive wall, some thirty yards out, when Jorg unleashed an unstoppable killer strike that left the visiting 'keeper with no chance. Goal . . . . . . with a capital 'G'!

Yes, indeed, the German had made his mark. Certainly, on the evidence of his first two seasons with Rangers, few would relish facing up to one of those free-kicks.

But, then again, that's life . . . . . . and the Hammer must fall.

THE HAMMER

Jorg Albertz thunders home Rangers first goal in the
3-1 victory over Celtic at Ibrox on 2nd January, 1997.

MUST FALL

ANSWERS

FUN QUIZ

1. Marco Negri (2) and Alex Cleland (3-1, v Hearts, 4.8.97). **2.** Marco Negri scored all five goals. **3.** Roma and Fiorentina. **4.** 7 0 v Dunfermline, 18.10.97. **5.** True. 76 goals – 12 more than Celtic. **6.** Jorg Albertz, with 10 goals. **7.** Aberdeen (3-3, 13.9.97). **8.** Charlie Miller (1-1, 27.8.97). **9.** Hearts (3-0, 25.4.98). **10.** Take your pick!

RANGERS IN EUROPE QUIZ

1. True. The European Cup Winners' Cup Final of 1961, when Fiorentina of Italy won 4-1 on aggregate. **2.** Bayern Munich. 1-1 in Germany and 2-0 at Ibrox. **3.** Mark Hateley and Ally McCoist. **4.** It was played in Malmo (Sweden) due to the fact that the East German team were refused visas to visit Great Britain. **5.** Rangers lost 6-1 (away) and 6-3 (at home). **6.** Jim Baxter. **7.** CSKA Moscow, FC Brugge and Marseille. **8.** Bayern Munich won 1-0. **9.** True. In Season 1987/88, Rangers reached the quarter-finals, following fine victories over both Dynamo Kiev (Russia) and Gornik of Poland. **10.** 11-0! 3-0 in Germany and 8-0 at Ibrox.

PHOTO FUN QUIZ

Page 45 – Ian Ferguson (top) and Maurice Johnston (bottom).

ACKNOWLEDGEMENTS

Designed by Douglas Russell and Lisa Russell.

Typesetting and Origination by Inglis Allen, Kirkcaldy.

Bound in Scotland by Hunter & Foulis, Edinburgh.

All photographs supplied by The Sun (Picture Editor: Mark Sweeney).

Every effort has been made by the publishers to ensure the accuracy of all details and information in this publication.

Printed and Published in Scotland by

INGLIS ALLEN

40 Townsend Place, Kirkcaldy, Fife, Scotland KY1 1HF.
Telephone (01592) 267201   Fax (01592) 206049 ISDN (01592) 646166
ISBN 1-89959-904-5 © Inglis Allen 1998. All rights reserved.